Spring Training

written and photographed by Henry Horenstein

Macmillan Publishing Company   New York
Collier Macmillan Publishers   London

Thanks to Erin Addison, Bruce Bogle, Francoise Bui, Anne Childs, Dorothy Crawford, Lisa DeFrancis, Jim Dow, Lottie Gooding, Russell Hart, Lauren Lantos, Genoa Sheply, Mark Starr, Jacquie Strassburger, Judith Whipple, Cecilia Yung, and the Boston Red Sox organization, in particular Dick Bresciani and Josh Spofford.

This book is for Adam, Anne, and Sam.

Macmillan Publishing Company
866 Third Avenue, New York, NY 10022
Collier Macmillan Canada, Inc.

First American Edition. Printed and bound in Hong Kong.
10 9 8 7 6 5 4 3 2 1

The text of this book is set in Plantin Light.
Some of the photographs in this book have appeared previously in *Parenting* magazine.
A Pond Press Book. Designed by Lisa DeFrancis.

LIBRARY OF CONGRESS CATALOGING-IN-PUBLICATION DATA
Horenstein, Henry. Spring Training. 1. Boston Red Sox (Baseball team)
2. Baseball – Training. I. Title. GV875.B62H67 1988 796.357'64'0974461
87-34842 ISBN 0-02-744440-6

Spring is a time of change. The weather turns warm. The days get longer. Flowers bloom. Birds fly north.

For some people, spring is a time to get out a rake and shovel and plant the garden. For kids, it's time to take off boots and winter coats and begin dreaming of summer vacation.

For baseball players, spring means the beginning of yet another season. It's time to go back to work. Of course, good players work all year round. Sure, they may take some time out to rest their injured and tired muscles. But those players who sit around all winter just watching TV and eating too much won't last long in the major leagues. It's important for baseball players to stay in shape the entire year. Therefore, most players exercise daily and watch their diets. Some players stay sharp by playing winter baseball in faraway places where the weather is warm, like the Dominican Republic, Mexico, Puerto Rico, and Venezuela.

The funny thing about spring training is that it takes place mostly in the winter. In late February, pitchers and catchers meet with their coaches and manager at a training camp in either Florida or Arizona, where it's warm enough in winter to play baseball. The rest of the players join them soon afterward.

Some kids visit spring training during spring vacation from school. Sometimes parents take them. Other times they get to go while visiting grandparents—there are a lot of grandparents in Florida and Arizona. Most people think this is because of the warm weather, but it may have a lot to do with all the baseball you get to watch there.

In this book, we'll follow the progress of one team—the Boston Red Sox—through spring training. We'll see them practice and play games against other teams both at their home in Winter Haven, Florida, and on road trips.

For a few weeks, spring training consists of team practice every day. Early in the morning before practice begins, the field is very still. The pitching mound and home plate are covered, to keep them dry and in good condition, in case of an overnight rain.

The practice sessions require a lot of hard work. To help them get in good physical shape, ballplayers run laps several times during the day. Laps are probably one of the least enjoyable parts of being a player.

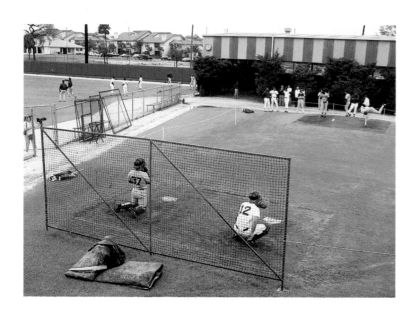 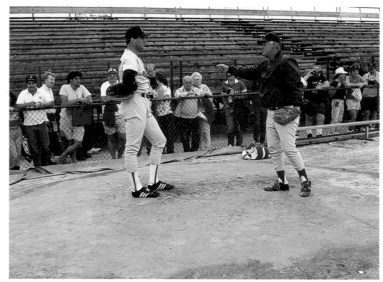

Then, with the help of coaches, players work on the skills required for the positions they play. In one of the areas where the pitchers and catchers practice, the net keeps balls that catchers miss from getting lost.

Even veteran pitchers like Bruce Hurst need help from time to time. The fans are so close to the action that they can hear everything the pitching coach is saying.

Coaches spend hours hitting balls to infielders and outfielders so they can practice their fielding skills.

Every aspect of the game must be taught and practiced—even running. Here, players watch a demonstration of the fine art of base stealing.

Certain dedicated Red Sox hitters take extra batting practice
every day with coach Walt Hriniak. From his sitting position,
Walt throws hundreds of pitches every day. The screen placed in
front of him protects him from the hit balls.

Catchers have to practice, too. The machine on the right
automatically tosses balls up in the air. The catcher gets into
catching position with eyes covered, and when the ball is tossed
up he has to find and catch it.

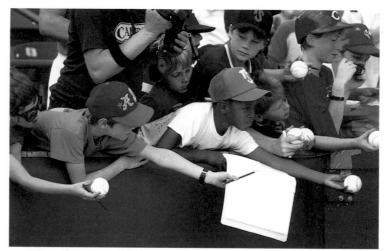

What many people like best about spring training is that, if you get lucky, you can get an autograph from your favorite player. You can almost always get an autograph from a rookie or a coach because not as many people ask them for one.

Newspapers, magazines, radio, television—everywhere you look,
players are being interviewed and filmed, especially stars like
pitcher Roger Clemens.

Two of the greatest Red Sox players ever, Ted Williams and Carl Yastrzemski, known as Yaz, come to spring training camp to help young players. Williams, who had a lifetime batting average of .344, talks things over with slugger Sam Horn, while Yaz stands behind the batting cage to get a better look at a rookie's swing.

Companies that make baseball equipment send representatives to all the spring training camps to provide the players with gloves, bats, shoes, and so forth. These companies hope that when fans see players using a particular brand, they will buy that same brand for themselves.

When practice is over for the day, the bats and other equipment must be gathered up and put away. This is done by the team batboys. Just about any kid would love to have this job; batboys are friendly with ballplayers and get to watch all the games close up.

After a few weeks of practice, the Red Sox begin the exhibition season. They play practice games with other teams that have training camps nearby. Exhibition games resemble regular season games in many ways, except they don't count in the standings and more young players get a chance to play and show off their talents.

For the first exhibition game of the season, there is a big crowd. Here, people drive their cars into the parking lot and wait in line to buy tickets.

The grounds crew makes sure that the playing field is in top shape for the game. These men are adding dirt to the infield to replace parts that have been dug up in practice.

For the first spring training game, the Cincinnati Reds come to Winter Haven. When he was a player, Pete Rose, the Reds' manager, had more major league hits than anyone else—more than 4,000.

Tape is sometimes used to prevent a favorite bat from breaking during hitting practice. The tape must be removed before the bat is used in a game.

The game begins, just as during the regular season, with our
national anthem. Everyone in the stadium stands up while "The
Star-Spangled Banner" is played.

Cincinnati Reds slugger Eric Davis has a powerful home-run swing, and he demonstrates it during the fifth inning of the game.

The next team to arrive in Winter Haven is the New York Yankees. They are very popular, and wherever they play, the stadium is sold out.

Don Mattingly, Yankee first baseman, warms up before the
game begins. He is one of the great hitters in baseball, and an
excellent fielder as well.

The Yankee pitcher also must warm up. He seems to be throwing strikes to his catcher.

Red Sox left fielder Jim Rice swings for the fences and hits a long double against the Yankee starting pitcher.

When the umpire runs out of clean baseballs, he asks the batboy to get some new ones. This kid isn't an official batboy; he has no uniform. He's just helping out for a while.

After the game, the manager meets the press. He answers
questions and tells them what he thinks of the game. The
reporters use this information, along with their own observations,
in the articles they write for the next day's sports page.

After several home games, it's time to visit other spring training camps. During spring training, teams travel on buses for road trips because almost all the teams have their training camps in Florida. During the regular season they fly on airplanes because they have to travel much longer distances.

The first stop is Grant Field in Dunedin, the home of the Toronto Blue Jays. This man is selling programs to fans as they walk into the stadium.

Playing professional baseball is hard work, even during
exhibition games. Notice the intense look on pitcher Oil Can
Boyd's face as he prepares to deliver a fastball to a Toronto hitter.

Safe at first—but just barely. Sometimes the runner takes too long a lead at first base and has to dive back to the bag to avoid being picked off.

The next away game is played in Orlando at Tinker Field against the Minnesota Twins. The Red Sox's slick-hitting third baseman, Wade Boggs, fields some ground balls before the game.

This fan takes time out from the game to enjoy some popcorn. For some reason, food at the ballpark always tastes great.

While waiting at the batting cage, players from the Red Sox and the Twins have a chance to stand around and chat. Most haven't seen each other since the previous season, so they discuss such things as their golf games and how their wives and kids are doing.

When the game begins, Red Sox outfielder Mike Greenwell is prepared as he sets to field a hard line drive.

Even though they are just practice, exhibition games are taken seriously. When the Red Sox manager disagrees with a call, he has a heated discussion with the umpire and is thrown out of the game. Another umpire leads him away and tries to calm him down.

Things can get pretty boring while waiting for the ball to be hit to the outfield. Stretching is a good way to keep loose and prepared between fly balls.

When the Sox travel to play the Detroit Tigers at Marchant Stadium in Lakeland, they get beaten badly. This Tiger runner is circling third for home.

Umpires have excellent vision, although not everyone thinks so. Still, they must dust off home plate several times during a game to call balls and strikes more accurately. This also helps the pitcher see where to throw the ball.

Soon after the trip to play Detroit, the Red Sox travel to Fort
Lauderdale to play a night game against the Yankees. In the late
afternoon, these Yankee players are stretching before working
out. This will help prevent muscle strains and other injuries.

Just before the game is set to begin, it starts raining. The grounds crew protects the playing field with a tarpaulin—a waterproof covering—to prevent it from becoming sloppy, which could cause a player to slip and hurt himself.

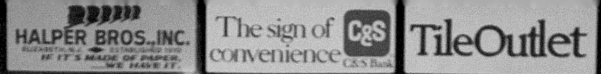

Once the tarpaulin is removed, a man in a cart drags a screen around the infield to smooth out the dirt so that balls hit on the ground won't take a bad hop.

While the field is being prepared, these Yankee players are doing sprints—short, quick runs—in the outfield. Sprints help them get loose and tuned up just before the game.

Next time you're at a game, watch good hitters, like Red Sox outfielder Dwight Evans, while they wait in the on-deck circle. They are always moving, practicing their swing or stretching their muscles, so they'll be prepared when it's their turn to bat.

After the Yankee game, the Red Sox are off to Vero Beach to play the Los Angeles Dodgers. Tommy Lasorda, Los Angeles Dodger manager, tips his cap to appreciative fans before the game at Holman Stadium.

Ray Dandridge, recently inducted into the Baseball Hall of Fame, throws out the first ball, and the game is about to begin.

Dodger players watch the game from an open dugout. The fans are close enough to the players to hear their strategy and even chat with them.

The Red Sox next travel to Al Lang Stadium in St. Petersburg, the spring training home of the New York Mets. Before the game, Mets players practice their fielding skills and have a little fun at the same time.

Mets outfielder Daryl Strawberry adjusts his wristband while sitting in the dugout and waiting for the game to begin.

The umpires go over the ground rules with coaches from the Mets and Red Sox. They discuss such matters as the boundaries between foul-ball and fair-ball territory. Since each stadium is built a little differently, it is important to review this information before each game.

One nice thing about baseball games is that soda and food, such as hot dogs and popcorn, are sold right in the stands. You can get a Coke without even leaving your seat. If you go to the food counters downstairs, you usually have to wait in line and end up missing part of the game.

This is the part of the game you don't want to miss. In the third inning the Red Sox have men on first and second with no outs.

The Red Sox win, 4–2. After the game is over, this Red Sox player, carrying his own equipment bags, waves good-bye to a friend on the Mets.

The Red Sox team bus also leaves immediately after the game is over. The players must wait until they get home to change clothes. Even though the game is played on the Met home field, a lot of Red Sox fans hang around to say good-bye and wish the team well.

Most of the fans leave the park and head for their cars right after the last out is made.

By early April spring training camp is over. The Red Sox fly north to Fenway Park to begin the regular season. While it's still fun to go to regular games, you have to sit so far away that you hardly get to see what the players look like. You never get to hear what they talk about, and it's really hard to get an autograph. That's why watching baseball at spring training is the best!